William Lyon Mackenzie King

#10

The loner who kept Canada together

Written by Nate Hendley

Illustrated by Jordan Klapman

Photo Credits
JackFruit Press would like to thank Martyn Devenyi for the photographs appearing on pages 3, 21, 27, 29, and 43; the Canadian National Archives for photographs on pages 9 (PA-146823), 23 (C-039555), and 41 (C-29464); Getty Images for images on pages 17 (Ed Clark, Time & Life Pictures), 35, and 33 (FPG/Taxi). Thank you to Foto Research for photographs on pages 27 and 37. We also wish to thank Bernard Roche, curator of Laurier House, Ottawa, for obtaining the image appearing on pages 19 and 21.
DISCLAIMER: Every effort was made to contact the owner of the photograph appearing on page 15 of this book. Please notify the publisher if there is a problem with the image.

©2006 JackFruit Press Ltd.
Author—Nate Hendley
Illustrator—Jordan Klapman
Beaver cartoons—S. Dan Morris
Publisher—Jacqueline Brown
Editor—Helen Waumsley
Designer and Art Director—Marcel Lafleur
Researchers—Peter Konieczny, Jason Lawrence, Barbara Baillargeon, and Hagit Hadaya

JackFruit Press Ltd.
Toronto, Canada
www.jackfruitpress.com

Library and Archives Canada Cataloguing in Publication

Hendley, Nate, 1966–
William Lyon Mackenzie King: The loner who kept Canada together / Nate Hendley; illustrator, Jordan Klapman.

(Canadian prime ministers: warts and all)
Includes index.
ISBN 0-9736406-1-8

1. King, William Lyon Mackenzie, 1874–1950—Juvenile literature.
2. Prime ministers—Canada—Biography—Juvenile literature.
3. Canada—Politics and government—1921–1930—Juvenile literature.
4. Canada—Politics and government—1935–1948—Juvenile literature.
I. Klapman, Jordan, 1958– . II. Title. III. Series.

FC581.K5H46 2005   j971.062'2'092   C2005-906478-1

Printed and Bound in Canada

...So, I'm here to show you around this really cool series of books on great Canadians.

This book tells the story of William Lyon Mackenzie King, Canada's 10th prime minister.

Some folks thought he was Canada's dullest PM. But he still managed to improve the lives of Canadians in major ways.

Contents

Hot topics

A political cartoon circa 1925
pokes fun at King's policies

In a nutshell

What sort of man shepherded Canada through some of the most catastrophic events this country has ever experienced? Our 10th PM. The man whose face appears on our $50 bill. The man many still think of as our dullest leader ever. But, as his life story shows, even a lacklustre man can bring about great changes.

Wily Willie, a dull leader for exciting times

Ruthless dictators clambered to power throughout Europe. The **Great Depression** swept across the globe. Bloody war raged around the world. And William Lyon Mackenzie King was prime minister through it all.

From 1921 to 1948, almost without a break, he guided Canada through some of the greatest challenges the world and our country had ever faced. Economies, communities, and families were shattered by the **stock market crash** of 1929 (imagine if you were so hungry that you had to line up in the street for a bowl of free soup). Society was shell-shocked when, only 21 years after "the war to end all wars," a second world war broke out (imagine if almost everyone you knew lost a brother, a husband, a father, or a best friend, and then it happened all over again). **Adolf Hitler** horrified the world (imagine if he had won).

What sort of man shepherded our country through these catastrophic events? A man who was wildly popular, always surrounded by people? Nope. William was a loner, a confirmed bachelor who generally preferred the company of his dogs to humans (he had three Irish terriers in a row, all named Pat). A man with the flash and dash of William's rebel grandfather, **William Lyon Mackenzie**? Nope. Our Willie was tubby and bland, ponderous and dull (in public, that is . . .)

The secret diary

Can William possibly be as boring as he sounds? Nope, although everyone certainly thought so when he was alive. But after he died, his secret diary was discovered—and you'll never guess who William had been hanging around with for all those years . . .

The dead. He spoke with them. In secret seances held in darkened rooms.

OK, so think about this man whose best friend was a dog, and who socialized with otherworldly spirits by night, then turned around and ran a country by day. What sort of decisions would you expect him to have made? Would you be surprised to find out he created the **social safety net** that Canadians in need still count on today (programs such as **family allowance**, **unemployment insurance**, and **old-age pension**)? That he urged legislation shortening the workday from 12 hours to 8? That he had been driven to end poverty and social injustice from his teens? That over 20 years before he was elected prime minister, he had done volunteer work in slums and published articles protesting sweatshops?

If you're thinking that William Lyon Mackenzie King was a strange, steadfast, complex man leading Canada through exciting, violent, world-altering times, you're absolutely right.

Want to know more? The words in bold are explained in the glossary at the back of the book.

Success can't fill the loneliness in William's life. On the night he wins leadership of the Liberal party, he walks to his neighbour's cottage and tells her, "I've just been made party leader and I have nobody to share it with."

The PM is a recluse whose closest friend is a dog. He spends most of his spare time landscaping his Kingsmere estate and installing fake Roman-style "ruins" in the woods and on the pathways. William runs the country by day and secretly socializes with otherworldly spirits by night.

1881

Seven-year-old Willie accompanies his father to a political meeting. The highlight is a speech by Canada's first prime minister, Sir John A. Macdonald.

Even though Willie is too young to understand what Sir John is talking about, he's impressed by the great man's presence and is thrilled by his first brush with politics.

Igniting a passion for social change

William was born on December 17, 1874, in Berlin, Ontario. Now called Kitchener, Berlin was a busy community of some 3,000 people. His parents, Isabel and John King, already had one child, a daughter named **Isabel Christina Grace**. They would later have two more children—**Janet Lindsey**, in 1876, and **Dougall Macdougall**, in 1878. They were devout Christian parents who enjoyed reading the Bible to their children and singing hymns with them. Their faith shaped William tremendously. For the rest of his years, he would believe that God guided him.

A family of rebels

William's father, **John King**, was a lawyer with a thick beard in the manly style of the day. In addition to having a good job and fine facial hair, King was a staunch supporter of the **Liberal party**.

King's mother, **Isabel Grace Mackenzie King**, was a tough, strong-willed woman with famous ancestors. Her father, **William Lyon Mackenzie**, was one of Canada's best-known rebels. He led an armed revolt, known as the **Rebellion of 1837**, against the small group of powerful rich folk who dominated **Upper Canada**. The revolt failed but William Lyon Mackenzie's spirit remained very much alive in the tales of his deeds that Isabel passed on to her son.

William was kept busy as a child. His mother and father enjoyed skating, sleigh riding, and camping with their children. When William was seven, he got to accompany his father to a political meeting. The highlight of the evening was a speech by **Sir John A. Macdonald**, the long-serving prime minister. Even though young Willie didn't really get what Sir John was talking about, the great man's presence impressed him and he was thrilled by his first brush with national politics.

In 1886, the King family moved to a new home, called Woodside, that was built at the edge of town. Woodside was a solid, 10-room brick house with five and a half hectares of wooded land—plenty of space for Willie and his siblings to shriek and holler and horse around in.

Fleeing for his life

When he wasn't playing with his brothers and sisters or doing chores, Willie liked to read, particularly history books, the Bible, and collections of poetry. Though he loved both his parents, he completely idolized his mom. William's favourite thing was to sit at his mother's knee as she spun stories about his grandfather's great fight against unfair government. His mother told him about his grandfather fleeing for his life after the rebellion sputtered out. Her voice filled with awe, she described her father's years of exile in the United States, his 11 months living in prison with common criminals, and his eventual return to Canada as a hero of the people. Such tales stirred William to the core, especially because he had been given his grandfather's name. Even at a young age, he felt a calling to make life better for people, as if this were his own special duty to the world.

William was almost 17 when, in 1891, he began his studies at the University of Toronto. At the time, Toronto had a population of 181,000 people, which made it a big, fast-growing city by 19th-century standards in Canada. It would be William's home for the next six years, while he got his first three degrees in economics, government, and law.

Rex and Bert

At university, William acquired yet another nickname—his fellow classmates called him *Rex* (Latin for "King"). Rex studied hard and said his daily prayers. He was also somewhat of a jock (hard to believe, considering how physically inactive he was later in life). Besides working out regularly at the gym, he played cricket and football. He also joined the debating club and became fast friends with a student named **Henry Albert Harper**. Bert, as Henry was nicknamed, became William's best buddy and constant companion. Rex and Bert liked to go for bicycle rides, read poetry out loud, study, or just generally hang out together.

Living in Toronto sharpened William's sense of social justice. Sometimes the future prime minister walked around deprived parts of the city to see first-hand how poor people lived. It couldn't have been a pleasant tour. He would have seen dirty children playing barefoot in the streets, old

Kids at school called Willie "the rebel," after his famous granddad.

Willie was proud of this rebel heritage —and got into fights with kids who made fun of it!

At university, William's classmates call him Rex (Latin for "King"). He studies hard, works out regularly at the gym, and plays cricket and football.

William also joins the debating club, where he meets a student named Bert (Henry Albert Harper). They become best buddies and constant companions. They go for bicycle rides, read poetry out loud, study, or just generally hang out together.

people bent and broken from a lifetime of tough labour, and people begging everywhere.

In 1893, he began keeping a diary that he'd write in for the rest of his life. "The chief object of my keeping this diary is . . . that through its pages the reader may be able to trace how the author has sought to improve his time," William wrote in one of his first entries. "Another object must here be mentioned and is this, the writer . . . may find great pleasure . . . in the remembrance of events recorded."

William graduated with his bachelor's degree in 1895, got a law degree in 1896, then began his first master's. He decided to extend his studies by taking courses at the University of Chicago, in the United States.

Making a difference in the world

In Chicago, William continued to care about the downtrodden. He volunteered at Hull House, an organization that helped people in poor neighbourhoods. Many of these people were immigrants struggling to make their way in the **New World**.

William was deeply affected by his experience at Hull House. Clearly, his rebel spirit had been awakened. Chicago's slums and the desperation created by such poverty would stay with him all his life. He now knew for sure one of the ways he could make a difference in the world.

Exposing the sweatshops

After returning to Toronto in 1897, he wrote a series of articles for a newspaper, the *Mail and Empire*. His stories exposed the terrible working conditions in Toronto sweatshops (cramped factories where workers sewed clothes for pitiful wages). Picture yourself having to stitch clothing in the boiler room of your school, jammed in with dozens of other people. Now think about working there for 14 hours a day, six days a week, 52 weeks a year, earning barely enough for food and a crummy place to live. William soon returned to the United States to earn a second master's degree in political economy at the world-famous Harvard University. But he stayed in close contact with his best friend, Bert. And he also enjoyed the attentions of young women—especially attractive ones! But he was reluctant to enter into a serious relationship just yet.

After graduating, William treated himself to a well-deserved break from studies with a trip to Europe, where he visited England, France, Belgium, and Germany. He'd won a travelling fellowship from Harvard to further his research into—yeah, you guessed it—the causes of poverty. As soon as he returned, he was offered a great job. The Liberal party had decided to start publishing a magazine called the *Labour Gazette* and they wanted William to be its editor. This was a great honour and he eagerly accepted the post. It was his first real job since finishing his studies.

It's hard for us to imagine how horrible those slums were, as slums like that don't exist in Canada or the United States anymore.

Thousands of people crammed into a handful of filthy buildings . . .

. . . with no clean water or central heating or fans in summer. Some people didn't even have indoor plumbing!

Poverty and social injustice

Although William had a comfortable life, he noticed that many people around him lived in grinding poverty. He saw how poor people worked hard just to put food on the table while others got all the benefits that life had to offer: food, clean water, clothes, medical care, education and, maybe more importantly, respect from other people.

At the time, the general attitude was that people were responsible for their own standard of living. This attitude was a leftover from the early days of the colony, when most people were pioneers living in small, rural communities. Back then, most people lived on farms and were able to produce almost everything they needed (like food, clothes, houses, and furniture). They traded for other necessities that they couldn't grow or make themselves, like shoes or medicine. Families were expected to take care of each other. In emergencies, neighbours all pitched in to help.

After Confederation, growing **industrialization** attracted people to the cities in search of wealth. Many discovered that they'd traded the relative security of the family farm for the insecurity of a job. People were now dependent upon a regular cash income because they couldn't make or grow what they needed. In cities across the country, people lived in overcrowded areas because it was less expensive and close to their jobs in the factories. People either worked for insanely low wages or couldn't find regular work. Having to accept charity was sometimes a family's last resort but it was humiliating because it was considered proof of personal failure.

By the end of the 19th century, some community leaders began to argue that governments should help citizens in need. William personally believed in social justice, which is the view that society must provide the conditions to allow all of its people to share in life's rewards and responsibilities. The first modern social security program was put into place in 1914. Trade unions and other groups made a public issue of the increasing number of accidents at work, and the result was the Workmen's Compensation Act of Ontario. Injured workers now had the right to claim a regular income. Ontario's example was soon copied by other provinces.

From this time on, federal and provincial governments, including William's, introduced program after program of assistance. Today our modern social-justice system attempts to leave the shame of charity far in the past and be respectful of Canadians' right to receive benefits—not just because they're destitute, and not just because they made contributions entitling them to benefits, but because they are citizens.

For more information about Canada's social security system, visit our website at www.jackfruitpress.com.

Extremely wealthy American businessman John D. Rockefeller has a reputation for being tough with his workers. He hires William to help deal with miners in Colorado.

As an adviser on industrial relations for Rockefeller's mines, William tries to improve working conditions for the miners. He's paid $20,000 a year—a huge salary for the time.

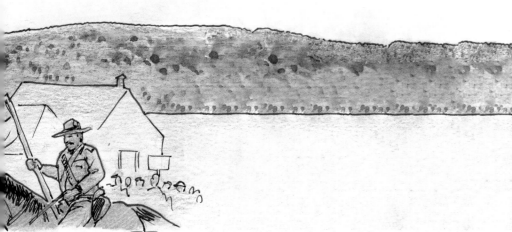

Willie gets a taste for power

While working for the Toronto *Mail and Empire* in 1897, William had written a series of articles on sweatshops. He'd been shocked to see the terrible working conditions there. He'd been even more surprised when he'd realized that the workers were sewing uniforms for Canada's postal workers! Rather than adding this tidbit of information to his newspaper article, William decided to tell the postmaster general (the head of the country's postal service).

The postmaster general asked William to check out the working conditions of any company that wanted to supply uniforms for postal workers. It was Willie's suggestion that the government insert a fair-wage clause into all future contracts. Prime Minister **Sir Wilfrid Laurier** made this clause part of the new law. Not bad for a beginner!

An enticing offer

William had barely settled into his editor's chair at the *Labour Gazette* when another enticing job offer came his way. Because of his work for the postmaster general, he was asked to become deputy minister of the federal government's new Department of Labour. William took the job and, at 25 years of age, became Canada's youngest-ever deputy minister.

1900
William is appointed deputy minister of labour.

1901
William buys Kingsmere.

His best friend, Bert Harper, drowns.

1906
William publishes his first book, *The Secret of Heroism*.

1908
Prime Minister Laurier urges William to run for office. He does, and wins.

1909
William obtains his law degree from Harvard.

He becomes Canada's first minister of labour.

1911
The Liberal party loses a federal election.

1914
William starts work for the Rockefeller Foundation.

World War I begins.

1916
William's father dies.

1917
William loses his seat in the federal election.

His mother dies.

1918
World War I ends.

William publishes *Industry and Humanity*.

1919
Sir Wilfrid Laurier dies.

William is chosen as new leader of the Liberal party.

In his new role, William got to do a lot of travelling. Among other duties, he regularly went around the country settling strikes. Strikes are settled by an independent listener (called an "arbitrator"). This person allows both sides to describe their problems (also known as grievances or issues). He or she then works with both sides (negotiates) to reach a solution that's acceptable to all. William quickly earned a reputation as a good listener and negotiator. Rich businessmen and poor workers alike trusted and respected him. They found him fair-minded and just. And William thrived in the job. Not only did he get to see the country, but his best friend, Bert, was working with him as assistant deputy minister! Having Bert around reminded him of all the fun times they'd had together at school.

Tragedy strikes

In 1901, William suffered one of the worst shocks of his life. While he was away from Ottawa, he read a newspaper article about a young man who had drowned in the icy Ottawa River while trying to save a drowning girl. William gasped in horror when he read the name of the dead hero. It was Henry Albert Harper!

William continued to work as deputy minister of labour. He did such a good job of settling strikes and investigating working conditions across the country that he attracted the attention of Prime Minister Laurier. Laurier knew a rising star when he saw one. He suggested that William join the Liberal party and run for office. William agreed and, in 1908, he won his first election and took a seat as a member of Parliament (MP).

Sir Wilfrid Laurier became a friend and continued to advise William. William's career moved ahead. In 1909, he received a doctorate from Harvard and became Canada's first minister of labour. In this role, he argued for radical ideas—radical for then—such as an eight-hour workday. People thought he was crazy! At the time, most working people got up at dawn and worked a 10- to 12-hour day with only a brief break for lunch.

A gloomy time

Only three years after William became an MP, the Liberal party was defeated in a federal election. William lost his **seat in Parliament**, which hurt him deeply. It was also a gloomy time for him personally. Both his mother and his father were ill and his younger brother, Dougall Macdougall, had developed tuberculosis. But, as had happened in the past, a new job suddenly brightened his prospects. In June 1914, he became director of the new Department of Industrial Relations at the **Rockefeller Foundation**, for which he was paid $20,000 (almost $500,000 today).

A couple of months after William took his job with the Rockefeller Foundation, war broke out in Europe. At 40 years of age, William was too old to

William was devastated when his best friend, Bert Harper, drowned in 1901.

In Bert's honour, a statue was built at the gates of Parliament. Called "Sir Galahad," after the Alfred Tennyson poem, it was unveiled in 1905.

A year later, William published a book about his buddy called "The Secret of Heroism."

Willie invents the company union

In the early part of the 20th century, one of the biggest issues in Canada and many other nations was the conflict between workers and employers. The men and women who worked in mines, on factory floors, or on construction sites often felt their wages were too low, their workdays too long, and their workplaces unsafe. They wanted to set up unions that would represent their interests. Their bosses, however, many of whom were wealthy, believed that employees should not be making such demands; nor would they deal with unions—if people didn't like where they worked, they could find another job somewhere else.

The struggle between workers and owners often turned violent, and governments would usually side with the owners in crushing unions and their strikes. One of the worst incidents happened in 1913, when 9,000 miners went on strike in Ludlow, Colorado, and the US government sent soldiers in to stop them. The result was a bloodbath, with over 40 people killed, including women and children. Many people across the United States were outraged by this and blamed the owner of the mine, John D. Rockefeller.

Rockefeller was the world's first billionaire, and he was very much against the idea of unions. But he needed help to solve his problems with his workers, so he turned to William, who had become an expert in this area. William put forward a compromise calling for company unions—where the company itself organized its workers into a union, but also controlled it. Workers could let it

know about their grievances and it would try to work out problems. William felt that it was the moral responsibility of owners to make sure their employees had a decent wage and safe working conditions. Rockefeller was won over by this plan and used it in many of his companies. By the early 1920s, hundreds of thousands of American workers were part of company unions.

William secretly believed that having company unions would lead owners to accept real unions. He was right about that. In the 1920s and '30s, many independent unions were formed and were grudgingly accepted by many companies.

Today, one can find unions for all sorts of workers, including teachers, nurses, and hockey players.

The struggle between mine workers and owners often turned violent

For more information about unions, visit our website at www.jackfruitpress.com.

Some folks called World War I "the war to end all wars" because they figured no one would be dumb enough to start another!

The whole thing had been horrible. Over 60,000 Canadian men were killed.

Although women didn't take part in combat, 56 of them were also killed. They were working as nurses on the war front.

And, at home, thousands of women were working in weapons factories. Many were poisoned by the chemicals used to make bombs or lost their lives when weapons accidentally exploded.

serve as a soldier. Spared the horrors of trench warfare, he went to work improving Rockefeller's image. Yet just as he was starting the job, several events gave him new reasons to feel sad. His older sister, Isabel, died in April 1915. His father died in 1916, apparently as a result of food poisoning. William was still grieving when his mother had a stroke (a sudden blockage or rupture of a blood vessel in the brain) in early 1917.

At the end of that same year, a federal election was called. This election was making Canadian history. For the first time, some women (those who had soldiers in their family) were allowed to vote. Although only some women got to vote, this was a breakthrough for women's rights.

The election was also important for William because he tried to make a comeback into politics. But in December 1917, William suffered two very hard blows. He lost the vote in his riding, which meant he couldn't return to Parliament as an MP. Then, one day later, his mother died.

A day to remember

The year 1918 proved to be a big one for the world and for William. On November 11 (now known as Remembrance Day), **World War I** ended in Europe. This same year, William published a book that he considered his life's work. Called *Industry and Humanity*, it talked about ways to improve ordinary people's lives. His most important political ideas were here in the book (for example, the idea that government should introduce old-age pensions, unemployment insurance, and greater medical coverage for the poor). It certainly helped boost William's profile across Canada. People liked his ideas, and he needed the recognition it brought because he was about to go after the highest job in the Liberal party.

William's friend and mentor, Sir Wilfrid Laurier, had died on February 17, 1919, so the Liberal party had to hold a political convention to select a new leader. Guess who they picked? William! He didn't have a seat in Parliament, but the delegates didn't care. The party soon found a vacant riding in Prince Edward Island that he could represent. That meant he could sit in the **House of Commons** again. William was delighted. He had managed to get back into politics at last.

Success, however, could not change one fact: he was lonely. There were no parties the evening he won the leadership; there was no one at home for him to rush back to tell. Instead, William walked to his neighbour's cottage and softly told her, "I've just been made Liberal leader and I have nobody to share it with." He returned to Ottawa in political triumph to become leader of His Majesty's Loyal Opposition.

Loneliness and the need for human contact

His personal diaries make it clear: William struggled with loneliness for much of his life. Most people who have studied William's biography say he was lonely because his mother meddled far too much. Others say he was lonely because he was unable to form deep and lasting relationships. Both are likely right.

For instance, when 22-year-old Willie was living in Chicago, he fell in love with a nurse, whom he dreamed of marrying. He wrote to his mother about it but she was firm in her disapproval. Her reply sternly reminded him of *her* dreams for *his* future. Willie came back to Toronto still single. In the choice between marriage and mother, Mom had won.

Throughout history, poems, stories, movies, and songs have talked a lot about loneliness. A Wordsworth poem says it all: "I wandered lonely as a cloud." So does a line from a pop song: "Saturday night is the loneliest night of the week."

But being alone is not always bad. In fact, there are times when being alone can be good for the soul. Time spent alone in deep thought can allow us to ask important questions, such as "Who am I? What's the purpose of my life?" Such questions are important and can really only be answered when you're alone and undisturbed by anyone else.

Of course, there are times when being alone can be painful. Like when you're suddenly alone because you've just lost someone you love. That loneliness is part of life and happens to everyone sooner or later. As unpleasant as it is, losing someone you love has to be accepted and lived through, one day at a time. For some of us, adopting a pet can help ease the pain of loneliness. That's what happened for William when he was given a dog.

Social loneliness is different. It happens when we're not able to find someone who makes us feel accepted and appreciated. When deprived of contact with others, most of us feel rejected. (Some psychologists say that we all need to be hugged at least seven times a day.)

The bust of William's mother, Isabel. William would pat it whenever he walked by.

Then there is aloneness. It's different from real loneliness because it arises from a decision to be alone. This is often the case with creative people, who need solitude for large chunks of time to explore and express their creativity. Their need for creative solitude can sometimes confuse other people, who worry that they're lonely.

In summary: don't hesitate to be alone whenever you feel the need. But being lonely is a situation that you can change if you want or need to.

Willie and Pat share
a moment together

For more information about loneliness, visit our website at www.jackfruitpress.com.

Having lost the election, the Liberals are expected to resign. But crafty Willie is determined to stay in power. To achieve this, he convinces two new parties to join him in forming a government.

Because he's lost his own seat in the House, William can no longer take part in debates. Frustrated, he watches the proceedings from the public gallery while his political cronies get hammered over a major scandal in the Customs Department.

Willie refuses to give up power

Things had changed a lot when William returned to Parliament as the new leader of the Opposition. Prime Minister **Robert Borden** had retired and the **Conservative party** had chosen a new leader. When William gazed across the centre aisle of the House of Commons toward the benches of the ruling Conservative party, he recognized the new prime minister—**Arthur Meighen**. William remembered him from his university days.

Meighen and William might have gone to the same university at the same time, but they sure didn't look or sound anything alike. Meighen was tall and thin, with a noble look, while William was somewhat short and rather dumpy-looking. Meighen was a brilliant speaker, quick with quips and insults. William spoke slowly, in a flat tone, and rarely said anything that people remembered.

A clever politician

William, however, had two huge advantages over the prime minister. First, he knew how to handle people much better than Meighen did. All those years William had spent settling strikes between bitter opponents had sharpened his ability as a peacemaker. Second, William was a clever politician who understood the kinds of issues that concerned voters. Meighen was smart but not nearly as good at the game of politics.

On December 6, 1921, William led the Liberal party to victory in the federal election. William became the 10th prime minister of Canada. But he didn't have long to celebrate. In March 1922, his younger brother, Dougall Macdougall, died as a result of the double whammy of

1919
The United States passes a law making alcohol illegal, but criminals import it by the truckload from Canada.

1921
Sir Wilfrid Laurier's wife dies and wills her home to William.

The Liberals come to power. William is Canada's 10th PM.

1922
William's brother dies.

Britain asks Canada for troops to fight a war in Turkey; William won't commit.

1923
William moves into Laurier House. He keeps this bust of his mother in the study.

1925
The Liberals lose the election by 17 seats. William loses his seat but forms a coalition that allows him to stay in power.

1926
William watches House of Commons debates from the public gallery.

The Liberals become involved in a scandal over alcohol smuggling.

William's party is forced to call a new election.

Meighen's Conservatives are asked to form a government but resign after only three days.

A new election is called. King's Liberals win with a majority.

William is PM for a second term.

21

Results of the 1921 election:

William Lyon Mackenzie King becomes Canada's 10th prime minister

Population:	8,760,211
Eligible voters:	4,435,310
Valid votes cast:	3,123,903

How the numbers stacked up:

Party	# votes	# seats
Conserv.	945,681	50
Liberal	1,272,660	116
Progres.	721,989	65
Other	183,573	4
Total	3,123,903	235

Issue: free trade vs. protectionism

tuberculosis and muscular dystrophy. Though deeply saddened, William had the responsibility of running a country to think about.

Prime Minister William continued to live a bachelor's life. Although he did date a few women, it was clear that no woman could be as good as his mother in William's heart. According to him, his mom was "the purest and sweetest soul that God ever made." William kept a statue of her in the house. He would even pat the statue and talk to it whenever he walked past.

Where there's a will, there's a way

In October 1925, a national election was held and the Liberals lost to the Conservatives by 17 seats. William was disappointed; he'd even lost his own seat. Still, always ambitious, he was determined to stay on as prime minister. But how could he do that when the Conservatives had the most seats?

Ever heard the phrase "where there's a will, there's a way"? William knew he needed a deal. He asked two smaller parties to join forces with the Liberals, and they agreed. This changed everything. The combined seats of the Liberals, the Progressives, and Labour now gave King more seats than the Conservatives. (This kind of arrangement is called a coalition.) Deal in hand, William had to get permission to form the government from **Governor General Julian Byng**. After a long discussion, Byng reluctantly agreed to the coalition. This meant that William could remain prime minister—for now.

Parliament returned in January 1926. Because William didn't have a seat, he had to watch the proceedings from the public gallery. No doubt he felt pretty embarrassed standing around with all those whispering and pointing tourists while his political cronies duked it out below. It wasn't an easy session to watch silently. And the Liberals sure could have used William's help, because the Conservatives were hammering them over a big scandal in the Customs Department.

Smugglers and bootleggers

Back in 1919, the United States had passed a law making it illegal to produce or sell alcohol (it was called "Prohibition"). In fact, very few Americans paid attention to the law. They wanted to drink alcohol and didn't care where it came from. This situation allowed many criminals in both Canada and the

How William bamboozled Byng

As the top political person in Canada, a prime minister has a lot of power. But that power can disappear quickly. For instance, in 1925, William called an election and his party lost to the Conservatives, led by his arch-rival, Arthur Meighen. William even lost his own seat, but still refused to accept defeat.

Instead, he invited the Progressive party to join the Liberals, then asked Governor General Julian Byng for permission to form a coalition government. After much discussion, Byng agreed.

Meighen was furious and decided to get back at William by raising a stink about a scandal involving the Customs Department. Some customs officials had taken bribes for allowing illegal shipments of alcohol into the United States. This had been going on for years, even when Meighen himself had been prime minister. But Meighen found a way to lay all the blame on William.

Meighen insisted that William resign for not preventing the scandal. He threatened to put the matter to a vote in the House of Commons; William would lose that vote and be forced to give up power. It would mean total disgrace. Never before had a prime minister been thrown out of office in this way. Our Willie, though, was too crafty to let such a vote go ahead. Instead, he went back to the governor general and asked permission to dissolve Parliament and call a new election. This time, Byng refused his request. William calmly went back to the House of Commons and announced that his government would have to resign—not because of the scandal, mind you, but because Byng had refused to dissolve Parliament.

Byng's role as governor general was to uphold the constitution. He believed that it was possible for Meighen to win the support of the majority of the House of Commons, whereas William had lost it. He also felt that, since Meighen's party had won the most seats in the election, he had to give him the same chance to form a government as he'd given William.

Pointing out that a governor general had never refused the advice of a PM in all the years since Confederation, William said that Byng's refusal made a mockery of Canada's Parliament. Because the governor general was officially a representative of the Queen, William argued that Byng's refusal made it look like Canada was still a colony, not a country in its own right. He then accused Meighen of disrespecting Canada's right to rule itself without intervention from England. Canadians agreed with William and returned him to power in the next election—with a majority.

Governor General Julian Byng

William's own philosophy was that a leader should do all he could to stay in power. Was William right to behave the way he did? After all, Meighen's own government had been just as involved in the scandal; he'd used it to try to defeat William and gain power. Some say this story shows that William was the better player; after all, there's nothing wrong with winning, is there? Or are there other ways of looking at the situation?

For more information about the King-Byng affair, visit our website at www.jackfruitpress.com.

United States to make a fortune selling illegal ("bootleg") alcohol. Canada also had Prohibition, but Canadian companies could make alcohol legally, as long as it was sold to foreign countries.

To get alcohol into the United States, smugglers paid Canadian customs officials to look the other way when they brought their booze over the border. For a long time, customs officers took bribes instead of seizing the liquor, or at least taxing it.

The Conservatives used this situation to embarrass the government. Customs officials bribed by criminals? This simply wouldn't do! While this scandal was unfolding, life in Parliament continued more or less as usual. For instance, a **by-election** had to be held in Saskatchewan to replace a minister who had resigned. This allowed William the opportunity he'd been looking for. By presenting himself as a candidate in that riding, he was able to get elected and take a seat in the House of Commons. To his relief, he could once again play an active part in the debates.

By late June 1926, things were really not going well for the Liberals. The scandal over alcohol smuggling was not going away. The Opposition called for a **confidence vote** (a vote that determines whether enough members of Parliament trust the government to continue to govern the country). Rather than allowing the vote to go ahead, William asked Governor General Byng to call an election. Byng said no. William resigned. Byng then asked Conservative leader Meighen to form a government.

Meighen's meltdown mode

William was not going to give up so easily. On June 30, he stood up in the Commons and asked if the members of Meighen's new cabinet had taken their oath of office. Of course, he knew that none of Meighen's cabinet had taken any oaths—they were only acting ministers and had not had time to go through all the proper procedures. Well, said William, then the Conservatives were breaking the rules!

Meighen went into meltdown mode. All parties began fighting about parliamentary rules and regulations. Government came to a standstill. The fight went on and on until finally, at 2 a.m. on July 2, the House of Commons took another vote. The Conservatives had 95 votes. The Liberals had 96. Meighen had lost a vote of confidence. There would have to be an election.

In the campaign leading up to the election, William pointedly accused the Conservatives of violating the rules of Parliament. He made it sound like it was the worst possible thing a Canadian could do. Many voters agreed. On September 14, 1926, the Liberals roared back into office! They won 116 seats, versus 91 for the Conservatives. Meighen was out and William was prime minister once more.

Some Canadians got quite rich by profiting from the sale of alcohol during Prohibition.

A US law makes it illegal to produce or sell alcohol in the United States. But thousands of Americans continue to drink illegal "bootleg" alcohol. Much of that booze is secretly imported from Canada.

Criminals smuggle booze into the United States. Canadian customs officers are taking bribes when they should be seizing the liquor, or at least taxing it. They're being paid to look the other way.

While many people believe that seances are a hoax, William frequently consults mediums to speak with the dead. He's convinced that the ghosts he chats with are genuine.

The lights dim. William holds hands with a group of fellow believers as a medium attempts to contact the spirits of deceased people. As usual, the PM will try to reach the ghosts of his parents or that of Sir Wilfrid Laurier.

Terriers and table tapping

As prime minister, William didn't do anything in a hurry. He often slept late, then read his Bible, and wrote in his diary before going to work. He'd conduct the nation's business from noon until 7:00 p.m. or so, then would retire for the evening.

Other times, his office hours could be quite erratic. He thought nothing of keeping his secretaries working past dinner or calling an assistant in the middle of the night to help him with a project. The prime minister didn't realize his staff had families and liked to keep normal hours. Having a wife and kids of his own might have made William more sensitive about other people's schedules. But he remained a bachelor who idolized his mother above all other women. This was unfortunate because, by the 1920s, he was mostly alone. Of his family, only his sister Janet was still alive.

Despite these losses, or maybe because of them, William didn't let many people get close to him. A Kingsmere neighbour who obviously held great fondness for William would later tell reporters how lonely he seemed, his home life filled with a love of poetry and spiritual hymns. His best friend was Joan Patteson, wife of a banker named Godfroy Patteson. Joan was older than William and might have reminded him of his mother.

Talking policy with Pat

In July 1924, the Pattesons gave William an Irish terrier as a present. The dog, whom he named Pat, soon became William's closest companion. He showered the terrier with affection, feeding him scraps from his dinner table and talking to the pup like a human. Some people said William liked to discuss policy issues with Pat as if the dog understood Canadian politics.

1924
William is given a dog, Pat, and becomes very attached to him.

1925
William meets with a fortune teller who assures him that she can contact his mom's spirit.

1927
The Liberals introduce old-age pensions to help protect the elderly against financial hardship.

1929
The New York Stock Exchange crashes. Not having lost any money, William thinks the crash is no big deal.

1930
Publicly attacked for being mean and petty, the Liberals suffer a major election loss.

Conservative leader Richard B. Bennett becomes Canada's 11th prime minister.

By the mid-1920s, William's public image was fixed. Most voters viewed him as a competent but dull leader. William's private life, though, was more colourful than anyone could have imagined! He was fascinated with psychics and the possibility of contacting dead people. William met regularly with a fortune teller named Mrs. Rachel Bleaney. Not only could Mrs. Bleaney predict the future, she was able to chat with the dead—or so William believed. William was amazed and delighted when Mrs. Bleaney got in touch with the spirit of his mom.

Talking to dead people

By the mid-1930s, William was regularly attending secret seances (gatherings in which people attempt to contact the dead) to try to speak with deceased family members. During these seances, William and a group of other people would sit around a table, often touching hands. The lights would be dimmed, then Mrs. Bleaney would mumble something. Her voice would suddenly change as if someone else was now speaking through her. Using Mrs. Bleaney as its channel, the "ghost" would talk about the afterlife or pass on messages to its loved ones. On other occasions, spirits would make their presence known by tapping on the table-top. This spooky stuff was often accompanied by mysterious music and other strange sounds.

Many people believed that seances were just hoaxes—and lots were. But some people believed that spirits really could be contacted. William was one of them; he was totally convinced his seances were genuine. He often held long chats with various ghostly presences, including his parents and Sir Wilfrid Laurier.

It's not clear whether William used seances to get political advice, but his diaries confirm that he asked the spirits about events in Canada and the world. Some historians believe he made major policy decisions based on what the ghosts had said. Others say William was more interested in hearing about his personal life, and ignored advice he disagreed with. William never talked about seances in public. If reporters knew about his mystical bent, they didn't write about it.

The calm before the storm

Following his re-election in 1926, all seemed well in Canada. The country was prosperous and flush with cash. Canada was now supplying half of the global market in wheat and more than half in newsprint. As part of William's plan to protect the elderly, his Liberal government introduced old-age pensions. Needy Canadians aged 70 years or older could receive $20 a month from the government.

Talk about going out of your way to get a doctor to do house calls!

In one of his seances, William asked the ghost of Louis Pasteur (the man who discovered that germs can cause diseases) to give him a prescription for his dog!

Spiritualism, seances, and communicating with the dead

William was by no means alone in his interest in seances and table tapping. Such practices were common among followers of the spiritualist movement, which flourished in William's time. After World War I, many grieving families had made desperate attempts to contact loved ones lost during the war.

Spiritualists believe that a person's spirit or soul remains alive after the physical body has died. Many religions share this belief. But spiritualists try to communicate with the inhabitants of the spirit world. In William's time, this communication was usually done by a medium (a person with well-developed psychic abilities) who performed in a group seance.

At the height of this period, people held seances in their homes or in spiritualist churches or meeting places. Many liked the idea of being able to communicate with deceased family members and friends. Some simply sought proof of life after death. Others explored the phenomenon scientifically and formed organizations to document their findings. Mainstream religious leaders frowned upon such practices. Skeptics dismissed spiritualism as a fraud that separated gullible victims from their money. Because this topic was so controversial, William never, ever discussed his otherworldly interests in public.

At a typical seance, spectral visitors (the spirits of dead people) would chat with the medium via telepathy (a way of sending mental messages without speaking). At other times, the spirit world would make its presence known by knocking on tabletops (table tapping), lifting objects (levitation), or making strange noises. But because these methods were easy to fake, hoaxes were a problem.

It's alleged that mediums with a strong connection to the dead emit "ectoplasm"—a dense type of energy that's supposed to enable disembodied spirits to take on visible form. This mysterious substance is said to be visible in the dark, and to disappear as soon as the lights come back on. Fraudulent ectoplasm has been proven, but other reports cannot be explained with our current level of understanding.

Since William's time, the spiritualist movement has grown in a wide variety of directions. These include tarot cards, psychic readings, and channelling. In more recent times, parapsychologists have studied psychic phenomena such as clairvoyance, telepathy, and telekinesis. Kirlian photography has produced images of the energy surrounding objects or living beings. Psi research has become a more respectable venture as it is reportedly now funded by the US and Russian governments in the hopes of creating psi spies!

While exploitation by crackpots remains a problem, research into the whole area is increasingly led by respected scientists dedicated to exploring unknown areas in pursuit of greater understanding.

For more information about spiritualism and seances, visit our website at www.jackfruitpress.com.

Hey! What happened to William's social conscience? What about all those things he wrote about taking care of the poor and the destitute? Was he being a hypocrite?

William didn't see it that way. As a politician, he was determined to stay in power. He felt that this was the most effective way for him to help those who needed assistance.

Besides, neither he nor Bennett appreciated just how bad things were and how desperate people actually were.

He thought that the situation was temporary and that it was the job of the municipal governments, not the federal government, to help the unemployed.

Many Canadians, however, looked to the stock market to provide a financial cushion for later years. The stock market allowed average citizens to buy shares of ownership in big companies. If the shares went up in price, they could be sold at a good profit. But if the shares went down, the stockholder could lose a fortune. By the late 1920s, the stock market in New York City (which set the pace for stock markets around the world) was climbing fast. Canadians and Americans were buying more and more company shares. But their actual value was dropping as prices rose.

Suddenly, on October 24, 1929, the New York Stock Exchange crashed (lost value). Overpriced stocks tumbled in value. Stockbrokers panicked and started selling shares at lower and lower prices . . . but no one was buying. Everyone wanted to sell. Right in front of their faces, stock prices bottomed out. The collapse of the New York Stock Exchange led to the global cataclysm called the Great Depression. It was a disaster. In North America and Europe, millions of people lost their jobs as countries and companies went broke. All the excitement and optimism of the 1920s came to an abrupt end.

For once, William's sharp political radar failed him. He didn't think the collapse of the stock market was a big deal, and believed that this temporary economic dip would correct itself.

Mean and petty

To help jobless people, municipalities handed out relief vouchers. These vouchers could be traded in for food, fuel, or rent. The provinces wanted the federal government to pay for the vouchers, but William didn't think that was a good idea. He didn't want the Liberal government to pay for any relief measures, including **unemployment insurance**. Nor would he help out in Conservative-run provinces. On April 3, 1930, he told the House of Commons that Ottawa would not give "a five-cent piece" to "any Tory government." His statement was repeated again and again in newspapers all across the country.

William later tried to explain what he meant, but it was too late. People were shocked at how mean and petty he appeared to be. Not surprisingly, the Liberals were thrown out of office on July 28, 1930. The Conservatives, under new leader **Richard Bedford (R. B.) Bennett**, took 137 seats, versus 88 for the Liberals. The Conservatives won because they promised to put the economy back on track. But how could they keep this promise if the economic collapse was a global problem?

By 1930, wheat prices had hit rock bottom and 200,000 Canadians were out of work. Canada was in the worst crisis of its young history.

To help jobless people, municipalities hand out relief vouchers that can be traded for food, fuel, or rent. The provinces want the federal government to pay for the vouchers, but William refuses to help.

Many Canadians decide to "ride the rails"—hop aboard railway cars and travel to other parts of the country in search of food or jobs. Beggars and homeless people begin appearing in all major cities.

1937

William meets with Hitler. The führer fools William, as he has fooled many other leaders. He pretends to be in favour of peace when he is really planning war. He pretends to be concerned about the well-being of all people when he is actually persecuting millions of his own citizens.

William writes in his diary: "Hitler smiled very pleasantly and had a sort of appealing and affectionate look in his eyes. My sizing up of the man was that he ... truly loves his fellow men and his country."

Depression, despair, and a dictator

William sulked as Opposition leader and wondered how voters could have turned against him. He seemed more upset by his own defeat than by the crisis swamping the nation. He continued to meet with psychics and paid little attention to the economic calamity that had befallen the world.

The ruling Conservative party didn't have this option. They also had very few ideas about how to deal with the Depression. The new prime minister thought the economy would fix itself. Like William, R. B. Bennett wanted to spend as little money as possible on relief efforts.

In 1930, the Conservatives passed the Unemployment Relief Act, which designated $20 million to help the jobless. William was appalled. From the Opposition benches, he criticized the Tories for "running wild with the taxes of the people" and conducting "an orgy of public expenditure." Yet, in reality, $20 million was a drop in the bucket. The country continued to sink deeper and deeper into the Depression.

To make things worse, the Prairies were suffering from severe drought and crop failure. As the once moist and fertile soil dried out, huge clouds of dust blew across the land. By the early 1930s, one-third of all municipalities in southern Saskatchewan had experienced crop failures. By 1933, 1.4 million Canadians—a tenth of the entire population—were totally unable to support themselves. Without the handouts (money and vouchers) given to them by provincial governments and local charities, many people would have starved.

Labour camps and Bennett buggies

Bennett set up labour camps in remote parts of Canada, where young men could get room and board and 20¢ a day for cutting trees and moving rocks. Life was harsh in the camps, which were run by the army. It was not until William toured the Prairies that he

1930
The Conservatives pass the Unemployment Relief Act to help the jobless. William says the Act is "an orgy of public expenditure."

1930s
Canada sinks deeper into the Depression.

In the West, huge dust storms cause massive crop failures.

1933
Thousands of young men live in labour camps run by the army. Thousands ride the rails in search of work.

1935
William is returned to power for a third term with the slogan "King or Chaos."

1936
Hitler takes power as the chancellor of Germany. His Nazi followers are jubilant.

1936
The CBC (Canadian Broadcasting Corporation) is created.

1937
William meets Hitler. Like many others, he's impressed.

1939
The Nazis invade Poland and start World War II.

finally got a more realistic understanding of just how bad things were.

Many Canadians decided to "ride the rails"—hop aboard railway cars and travel to other parts of the country in search of food or jobs. Beggars and homeless people began appearing in all major cities. Farmers couldn't afford gasoline, so they hooked their cars up to horses to get around. People called these contraptions "Bennett buggies" after the increasingly unpopular prime minister.

Voters quickly became fed up with the Conservatives' inability to end the economic downturn. In October 1935, William and the Liberals easily swept back into office. Their campaign slogan was "King or Chaos"; they'd vowed to close the labour camps and improve the economy.

Depression over, war begins

It was William's third term as prime minister. His timing was good because the worst of the Depression was over. William saw that it was a perfect opportunity to act on the ideas he had written about in *Industry and Humanity*.

His first step was to make changes in the way Canada was governed. According to the **constitution**, provincial governments were responsible for all the programs that cost a lot of money: education, health care, and caring for the poor. But the federal government was the only one with the power to raise the kind of money that such programs required. William had these laws changed so that the federal government could now carry out the type of social reforms he planned.

As a result, the federal government started providing unemployment insurance but the provinces were left with the responsibility of other programs that would help people, such as caring for the poor, education and health care. Because those programs were very expensive, the federal government would give the provinces the cash they needed.

William's government faced another important challenge during this difficult time: many people feared another war would break out in Europe. Adolf Hitler had taken power in Germany. In June 1937, William visited Germany and met with Hitler. He came away impressed and wrote about the German tyrant in his diary. The führer had fooled William, just as he had fooled many other world leaders. Hitler pretended to be in favour of peace when he was really planning for war.

By mid-1939, Hitler had taken over Austria and Czechoslovakia. Now he was threatening Poland. On September 1st, the Nazis invaded Poland. In response, Britain and France declared war on Germany. **World War II** had begun.

Before the Statute of Westminster was passed, in 1931, any time England went to war with a country, Canada did too.

This wasn't the case during World War II.

England went to war with Germany on September 3, 1939. William's government, however, waited until September 10, when the House of Commons could vote on it.

Fascism: A powerful idea gone bad

Ideas can be far more powerful than people realize. **Fascism** was such an idea. It's based on the belief that one's country or people should be respected above all others, and that if a country is going to succeed, everyone has to be committed entirely to it. Sounds like an appealing idea, right? After all, isn't that what nationalism is about? But some ideas turn bad.

Fascism came into being after World War I. It was a time when the world was changing quickly and many people were scared that things were getting out of hand. People were also trying to figure out why the war had been so terrible. Quite a few people believed that all governments, even those that were democracies, had become corrupt and useless. They felt that a drastic change was needed to make things better.

Benito Mussolini was one of the politicians to offer the kind of drastic change that appealed to so many people. He first started spreading his ideas as an Italian newspaper editor before the start of World War I. Although Italy had won the war, fighting had been very difficult. Many Italians felt that their country had failed them. Soon after, Mussolini and others started a new political party that called for Italy to become a Fascist state. Their idea was that Italy could become a great nation but, to do so, all Italians had to commit themselves to one way of thinking and one inspiring leader.

Mussolini's slogan was, "Everything in the State, nothing outside the State, nothing against the State." Those who did not agree with this idea were branded enemies and removed immediately.

Fascists took power in Italy in 1922. (Fascist states were also set up in Spain, Portugal, and Germany.) The German Fascists, known as Nazis, were led by Adolf Hitler, whose views were even more extreme. Hitler believed that Germans were a superior people who should rule all others. Citizens of countries like Poland and Russia were considered only good enough to be slaves, while Jews and Gypsies were accused of not even being human.

Fascists first pretended to support democracy but, once in power, they banned political parties, stopped having elections, and made their leaders into all-powerful dictators. At first, it looked as if Fascism were indeed a good solution. There were no more strikes and all other forms of dissent stopped. To increase the impression that things were much better, Fascist governments in Italy and Germany perfected **propaganda** (misleading information used to promote a belief or cause). All problems were blamed on foreigners, Jews, homosexuals, and anyone else not committed to "The Cause." Undesirable individuals were either killed on the spot or sent to concentration camps where they were quietly eliminated.

As Mussolini and Hitler became more powerful, they each started to expand their empires. Italy invaded North Africa while Nazi Germany took over

Joseph Goebbels salutes in that special Nazi way

several countries in Europe. Their aggression eventually triggered World War II as other nations, including Canada, joined forces to stop the Fascists from expanding any further. After Germany and Italy were defeated, and Mussolini and Hitler met their end, the world was left with the task of repairing the damage caused by Fascism, the powerful idea that turned really bad.

For more information about Fascism, visit our website at www.jackfruitpress.com.

1943

Canadian troops land in Sicily as the first step in a larger invasion of Italy. The fighting is tough but the Canadians fight valiantly and distinguish themselves in action.

Later in 1943, Canadian soldiers take part in a vicious battle in Ortona, Italy, as the Allies move up the Italian "boot."

Dieppe, D-Day, and the draft

Shortly after Germany attacked Poland, William took part in a seance. A spirit informed the prime minister that Hitler was dead, killed by an angry Pole. This was reassuring to William, who dreaded another bloody world war. Could it be stopped? The prime minister had quite a shock when he left the seance and discovered that Hitler was still very much alive. Canada declared war on Germany on September 10, 1939.

At first, William thought Canada's role would largely consist of sending manufactured goods and natural resources, not soldiers. He promised the House of Commons that he wouldn't introduce overseas conscription; Canadian boys, he vowed, would not be drafted to fight in Europe. He could not forget that over 60,000 of them had died helping Britain in World War I. Much as he wanted to help Britain this time, he was worried about upsetting Quebec, which was strongly opposed to conscription. William listened carefully to his advisers on the issue. With the tyrant Hitler as an enemy, however, this was not turning into an ordinary foreign war.

1939
Hitler invades Poland.

Bitterly disappointed with Hitler, William finally agrees to declare war on Germany.

1940
The Nazis invade Belgium, Holland, Norway, and France.

In Britain, new prime minister Winston Churchill vows to resist.

William wins a new election with a large majority.

William's government passes the National Resources Mobilization Act.

1941
Pat (William's first dog) dies. William is devastated but soon replaces Pat with another terrier (like this one) named Pat II.

Visiting Britain, William is booed by Canadian troops waiting to get into combat.

Japanese planes bomb Pearl Harbor. The United States finally joins the war.

Canadian troops suffer massive casualties at the hands of the Japanese army in Hong Kong.

1942
Six thousand Canadian soldiers take part in a disastrous "test invasion" of Dieppe, France.

37

William had won the 1940 election partly because he had promised not to force Canadians to fight in a foreign war.

Once he realized that Canada could not stay out of the war, he asked the Canadian people to release him from that promise.

He told the people that his government would consider "conscription if necessary but not necessarily conscription."

This vague promise worked well. The English-speaking population thought Canada would definitely send troops to war. But the French-speaking population believed it meant they wouldn't have to fight if they didn't want to.

Holding Canada together

William was terrified of reopening old divisions between the English and the French. He had visions of chaos erupting across Canada—chaos that would lead to open warfare, death, destruction, and hatred. He was convinced that he was the only one who could hold Canada together and prevent civil war.

Even though the debate over conscription caused bad feelings, the advent of war was good for the economy. The government had always spent as little as possible on the military; until the late 1930s, the Canadian army did not own a single tank. Now, the armed forces expanded at a rapid clip, opening up a sea of jobs for young men. Ottawa began spending enormous amounts of money on war equipment. Nothing was too good for the brave Canadian lads who volunteered to fight Hitler's tyranny. By the fall of 1939, people had real jobs they could be proud to perform.

On March 26, 1940, William was easily re-elected prime minister, partly because he had promised not to introduce conscription. A few days later, he appointed Clarence Decatur Howe as minister of munitions and supplies. Howe more or less took over the economy. Factories began turning out planes, tanks, and guns instead of cars, fridges, and stoves.

A dark and frightening turn

In the spring of 1940, the war in Europe took a frightening turn. After pausing for several months following their invasion of Poland, the Nazis rolled over Belgium, Holland, Norway, and France. The German forces smashed any army that opposed them. British and French troops scrambled to escape to England. It looked like Britain itself would be invaded.

Back in Canada, it was dawning on William that the country couldn't get away with just providing supplies and raw materials. The Nazis had proven to be far more powerful than anyone had anticipated. It would take a huge effort to stop the German war machine.

"It is now left to the British peoples and those of British stock to save the world," William wrote in his diary. Then, on June 21, 1940, the National Resources Mobilization Act was enacted. The act drafted young men into the army, but only for duty in Canada, not Europe. This way, William could say he lived up to his promise not to draft anyone into overseas duty.

As a result of the mobilization act, Canada found itself in charge of two separate armies: conscripts who were based at home (called "reserve" men) and volunteers who would fight abroad ("A" men). This wasn't a very efficient way to fight a war, but William was determined to appease Quebec and avoid a conflict he felt would plunge Canada into civil war.

How Canada neglected to help Jewish refugees

When the Nazi party started to persecute Jews, it was cheered by anti-Semitic groups around the world. And Canada was not immune to racial hatred. In Quebec, ultra-nationalists took out their rage against Jewish children, families, and shopkeepers.

In 1939, after German and Austrian Jews had been sent to concentration camps, the St. Jean Baptiste Society presented the Canadian government with a petition bearing 127,364 signatures. The petition opposed immigration of any kind, especially Jewish. When it came to immigration, Canada's policy was that it was a British country and people wanted to keep it that way. In the 1920s, official "desirability lists" placed British immigrants at the top and then, in descending order, German, Scandinavian, Dutch, and French. These were the "chosen races"; then came eastern Europeans, Asians, and blacks. Allowed unwillingly were British Jews; other Jewish refugees' applications were handled on an individual basis called "special permit," with decisions made by an immigration official.

People speaking of pre-World War II days might argue that Canada could not permit immigration from Europe because citizens would lose their jobs to newcomers. Before the Depression, it was obvious that, whether through poor judgment or feelings of racial superiority, William and his government felt more secure by keeping Jews out of Canada. Sadly enough, this anti-Semitic, "closed door" policy was supported by a majority of Canadians. Meanwhile, Hitler was amassing tanks and armour near the German borders of many European countries.

Just when Jews most needed sanctuary from the forces of Nazism, sanctuary was denied. The Canadian bureaucrat in charge of saying no was a man named Frederick Charles Blair. Blair saw himself as a loyal civil servant getting it straight from the book. He didn't trust Jews, he didn't like Jews, and he was proud of the number of Jews he turned away. When Jewish Canadians promised to pay passage and then support any Jews that Canada allowed in, Blair accused them of lying. When asked to accept orphans, he refused on the grounds that they were not really orphans and would use their status in Canada to try to get their parents in.

Canada rejected Jewish millionaires with money to invest, well-educated businessmen, academics, and scientists. One Canadian immigration officer in Europe had cleared hundreds of Jews for entry into Canada, only to have "Blair's Blockade" refuse them. They were all rounded up and executed by the Germans.

As late as 1943, there was still a chance to get 6,000 children out of France before the Gestapo collectors arrived. The Canadian Jewish Congress had already promised sponsorship. The United States offered 4,000 visas and asked Canada to take 1,000 of them; Canada didn't respond. Blair was never accused of a crime. He was doing what so many others did at the time—he was following orders. The Jews had been abandoned to the Holocaust.

For more information about the Holocaust, visit our website at www.jackfruitpress.com.

39

In July 1941, William's Irish terrier and beloved best friend, Pat, died. William was devastated. Travelling to Britain for a series of meetings, he adopted another Irish terrier, whom he named Pat II. In a public speech, he said, "If I have been true to some of the great causes . . . it's been the example of that little fellow that has helped in many, many ways."

Attack on Pearl Harbor

On December 7, 1941, Japanese planes attacked the US navy in Pearl Harbor, Hawaii. The United States never thought the Japanese would attack it before officially declaring war. Most of the United States' biggest warships were docked at Pearl Harbor, and a number of airplanes were housed there too. The Japanese sank just about every important ship in the US Pacific Fleet. The American public was shocked; the United States declared war on Japan, officially joining the **Allies** in their fight against the Axis powers.

The expanded war sparked feelings of racial hatred against Japanese Canadians, many of whom had been born in Canada and lived in British Columbia. It was feared that they might spy for Japan or commit acts of sabotage. In early 1942, William signed an order authorizing the forced internment of Japanese Canadians. (Germany and Italy were also "enemy nations," but a much smaller number of German and Italian Canadians were interned.)

On August 19, 1942, Canadian troops stationed in England finally saw action. That day, a force of some 6,000 men—the majority of them from Canada—attacked the French seacoast town of Dieppe. The Germans had fortified their defences well. Nearly 1,000 Canadian soldiers were killed; many others were wounded or taken prisoner. Survivors who made it back to the beach were rescued by Allied ships waiting offshore.

Canadians fighting bravely

Canadian forces fared much better in other military operations. In 1943, the Royal Canadian Air Force (RCAF) got its own unit, separate from the British Royal Air Force (RAF). RCAF bombers regularly flew dangerous missions over occupied Europe. Canadian troops landed in Sicily as the first step in a larger invasion of Italy. Canadians fought bravely and distinguished themselves in action.

In August 1943, William, British prime minister Winston Churchill, and US president Franklin D. Roosevelt met in Quebec to discuss the war and outline plans for the future. William was delighted to host these conferences. But he was a lot less enthusiastic when it came to dealing with the issue of conscription. By 1944, the reserve army had grown to 70,000 men. As the war progressed, Canadian military leaders urged William to send these men to Europe as reinforcements. The prime minister stalled, but, as he dithered, the call for reinforcements grew louder and louder.

War is hell. The numbers speak for themselves . . .

Canada: 42,042
Belgium: 88,000
Netherlands: 200,000
United States: 300,000
Britain: 400,000
Hungary: 400,000

Italy: 400,000
France: 600,000
Yugoslavia: 1.5 million
Japan: 2 million
Germany: 5.5 million
Poland: 6 million
China: 10 million
USSR: 20 million

That's how many people were killed in World War II.

40

Canada's Japanese wartime internment camps

The declaration of war on Japan had a huge impact on the 23,000 people of Japanese descent who were living in Canada at the time. Most Japanese Canadians were either naturalized citizens or Canadian-born. Some came from families who had been living in Canada since the late 19th century. They had no desire to fight for Japan.

But none of this mattered to a public inflamed with hatred against all things Japanese. This hatred grew even stronger after Japanese soldiers massacred Canadian troops in Hong Kong.

Many people thought Japanese Canadians were going to commit acts of sabotage or espionage. They demanded that their elected representatives do something about this threat.

In January 1942, Japanese men between the ages of 18 and 45 were removed from the coast of BC and sent to isolated **internment camps**. A month later, Ottawa ordered the roundup of some 21,000 remaining Japanese Canadians. Most able-bodied men were sent to work camps in Ontario and Alberta. Old men, women, and children were interned in small towns in the interior of BC.

The federal government seized major assets (including farms, fishing boats, property, and businesses) belonging to Japanese Canadians. These assets were sold at a fraction of their real value to pay for their own internment, with only some of the proceeds going back to their rightful owners.

The public supported such moves; over half of the respondents to a 1943 survey said that Japanese descendants should be shipped back to Japan, even if they were born in Canada. No one cared that Japanese Canadians hadn't actually committed any acts of sabotage.

The end of World War II should have meant an end to the persecution of Japanese Canadians, but it didn't. While they were finally allowed to leave the internment centres, Japanese Canadians couldn't live within 140 kilometres of the Pacific Ocean, practise law, or take out commercial fishing licences. They couldn't vote in federal elections or in some provincial elections.

To Canada's shame, these blatantly **racist** laws were kept in force until 1949. It took decades more for Ottawa to make amends to the Japanese-Canadian community. In 1988, Prime Minister **Brian Mulroney** formally apologized for the treatment of Japanese Canadians during World War II. As compensation, the government gave $21,000 to every survivor of the wartime detention.

An internment camp for Japanese Canadians: a dreary village at the foot of the Rockies

For more information about internment camps, visit our website at www.jackfruitpress.com.

In a controversial decision to shorten the war with Japan, the United States uses a horrific top-secret invention, the atomic bomb, on the city of Hiroshima.

The bombing of Hiroshima kills approximately 90,000 people. Three days later, a second atomic bomb is dropped on Nagasaki and another 75,000 people are killed immediately. Thousands more will soon die or become ill from injuries and radiation poisoning. Japan surrenders. World War II is now officially over.

The war finally ends

1945
The war in Europe ends on May 7.

The war with Japan ends after the United States bombs Hiroshima and Nagasaki.

1947
Canadian Citizenship Act goes into effect. William becomes the first official Canadian citizen.

1948
William retires and starts to organize his papers and diaries and plan his memoirs.

William celebrates his 21 years in office as PM. His is the longest term in power for any elected leader of an English-speaking country.

1949
Newfoundland becomes Canada's 10th province.

1950
75-year-old William dies of pneumonia. He is buried in Toronto's Mount Pleasant Cemetery.

On June 6, 1944, 130,000 men—including 15,000 Canadians—landed in Normandy, France, as part of the massive **D-Day** invasion to bring the war into the heart of Nazi Germany. Canadians landed at Juno Beach and had to fight fiercely against German defenders.

The full extent of Hitler's holocaust was finally being uncovered. Allied forces liberated the first of his **concentration camps** in the spring of 1944. They were horrified beyond words at what they found: barbed-wire-enclosed barracks where innocent people were imprisoned in torturous conditions, starved, brutalized, forced to perform hard labour, and murdered. All because the Nazis didn't like their religion, race, politics, or opinions.

The fall of the Third Reich

By the fall of 1944, the Canadian army in Europe desperately needed more men. Casualties were high, and there were so few replacements that Canadian soldiers who had been wounded twice were being sent back to the front after recovering. Army generals said they needed at least 16,000 additional soldiers. On October 19, 1944, William told his cabinet that the reserves had to go to war. Of a total of 12,908 men selected, only 2,500 actually made it to the battle zones by the spring of 1945. As the war drew to a close, Canadian forces pushed into occupied Holland. The Dutch people were overjoyed, and hailed the Canadians as heroes.

43

Nazi Germany finally surrendered on May 7, 1945. Hitler had killed himself the week before. The once-mighty **Third Reich** was no more. But for the 11 million innocent people murdered by the Nazis, peace arrived too late. General Dwight D. Eisenhower (the top US military leader) ordered journalists to take pictures and write stories about the camps so everyone around the world would know what these people had suffered.

All across North America, people danced and cheered in the streets. Though the war with Japan was still ongoing, people were delighted that the war in Europe had finally ended.

On June 11, 1945, a conference was held in San Francisco to launch the **United Nations** (UN). It was hoped the UN would become a group representing all the countries of the world and could peacefully resolve issues between nations. William happily signed the UN charter as the representative from Canada.

Dropping the bomb

While the war in Europe was over, Japan continued to fight on. In fact, the closer US troops got to Japan, the hotter the Japanese resistance became. The United States thought it would win, but was worried about the price it would have to pay in deaths if it invaded Japan.

The United States made a controversial decision. Instead of invading Japan, it used the atomic bomb, a top-secret invention that had never been used before. This horrific weapon pulverized the entire city of Hiroshima, killing about 90,000 people in one single explosion.

Three days after the bombing of Hiroshima, a second atomic bomb was dropped on Nagasaki. Approximately 75,000 people were killed immediately. Thousands more would soon die or become ill from radiation poisoning and other injuries. The frightening consequences of the bombing of Hiroshima and Nagasaki were so terrible that no one has ever used an atomic bomb in a war again. Japan surrendered and World War II was now officially over.

A heavy toll

By war's end, over 500,000 Canadians had served in the air force, army, and navy at a time when only 10 million people lived in the whole country. That's one in 20 people. For all the cheering and celebrations, the price of victory had been high: 42,042 Canadians were killed in World War II.

Germany surrenders one week after Hitler nits suicide. The mighty Third Reich is no . The war in Europe has come to an end.

Everyone is delighted that the carnage in Europe has finally stopped. All across North America, crowds dance and cheer in the streets. As with most major cities in Canada, a massive celebration takes place in downtown Toronto.

In the summer of 1945, Ottawa paid out the first family-allowance benefits. All households with children under 16 received small payments from the government. Later, William's government provided grants to the provinces so they could implement his policies on health and health insurance.

William's last term in office was fairly calm, though the United States and the USSR (now Russia)—former allies in the fight against Germany and Japan—did grow suspicious of each other. This state of affairs was called the "**Cold War**" because the United States and the USSR never actually engaged in direct combat with each other, but a real (or "hot") war was an ever-present threat. Both sides spied on each other, amassed stockpiles of nuclear weapons, and engaged in several "minor" conflicts (such as the Korean War) in which each country flaunted its ever-more sophisticated weapons.

Rex calls it a day

In the summer of 1947, Pat II died. William cancelled a cabinet meeting to stay home with the dying dog, rocking him in his arms while he sang hymns to him. In 1948, William celebrated 21 years in office—the longest term in power of any elected leader of an English-speaking country. William finally retired from office on November 15, 1948, at the age of 74. In his retirement, William adopted yet another Irish terrier, whom he named Pat III.

William spent most of his time at Kingsmere sorting through thousands of papers and secret diary entries in the hopes of organizing them into a memoir, but he never got around to finishing it. Can you see him sitting in his garden, or his ruins, and just remembering? He died of pneumonia at his Kingsmere estate on July 22, 1950, at 75 years of age. William was buried in Toronto's Mount Pleasant Cemetery.

He kept Canadians united

So who was this man who led Canada through some of the toughest moments of the 20th century? William Lyon Mackenzie King was tubby and bland, uninspiring and dull. Most of his speeches were so boring that hardly anyone could remember them—right after he'd finished talking.

By his own admission, William's most important contribution was not what his government did but what it prevented. And what exactly did it prevent? For a start, it stopped Canada from sliding into anarchy or dictatorship during the Great Depression. This was a very real fear at the time (look at what was happening in Nazi Germany and Fascist Italy!) During World War II, William kept Canada united in spite of a massive French and English division over conscription.

William still holds three distinct records.
1: He remains Canada's most educated prime minister.

2: He served as prime minister for more years than any other Canadian PM.

3: He served in office longer than any other elected leader in the English-speaking world.

His two most important features were his capacity to sense of what voters wanted and his willingness to make whatever changes were needed to stay in power. His government passed progressive legislation like old-age pensions, family allowances, unemployment insurance, and better health care for the poor and elderly. These laws later became known as the "social safety net"—programs now seen as sacred trusts of the Canadian way of life.

> "In politics, one has to do as one at s in a sailing ship; not try to go straight ah but reach one's cour. having regards to th prevailing winds."

As far as his "warts" go, we've seen that William's major handicap was his inability to form relationships. After his family was gone, all of William's affection went to his dogs. Loneliness was his lifelong complaint. He never experienced the simple happiness that most people enjoy every day. Though financially rich, William was poor in terms of emotional wealth.

Some people think it was William's inability to feel for others that made him insensitive to the fate of European Jews fleeing Nazi genocide and the sufferings of Japanese Canadians treated as spies in their own country.

While it's easy to blame William now for his insensitivity and intolerance, we have to remember that Canadians went along with it by keeping him in power for almost 22 years.

William might have been dull and grey but he was good at managing people, and he was a smart politician. He knew how to appeal to the self-interest of average Canadians. Never flashy or exciting, he was a steady, moderating presence—a familiar, comfortable figure that voters put back into office, again and again.

Is there more to William's legacy? Possibly. If there is, it might still be hidden in his diaries. William is just as much a mystery today as he was when he began to write his secret thoughts down, then hide them from the world.

47

Timeline: The life and times of William Lyon Mackenzie King

YEAR	WILLIAM'S LIFE	EVENTS IN CANADA AND THE WORLD
1874	William is born in Berlin, Ontario, on December 17.	The Liberals win a majority government in the federal election of January 22.
1875		The Supreme Court of Canada is established. The Indian Act is passed.
1876	William's sister, Janet Lindsey, is born on August 27.	
1877		Manzo Nagano is the first official Japanese immigrant to Canada.
1878	William's brother, Dougall Macdougall, is born on November 11.	John A. Macdonald is elected for a second term as prime minister. The Canada Temperance Act is passed.
1880		Edward Hanlan, a rower, is Canada's first world sports champion. Emily Stowe becomes Canada's first female doctor.
1885		The Canadian Pacific Railway is completed. Canada's first national park is created in Banff, Alberta. The Northwest Rebellion takes place; Louis Riel is hanged. The federal government imposes a head tax of $50 on Chinese immigrants.
1888		The first election takes place in the Northwest Territories.
1890		The Manitoba School Act is passed.
1891	William begins studying at the University of Toronto.	Sir John A. Macdonald dies while in office. John Abbott becomes the third prime minister.
1892		Sir John S. D. Thompson becomes the fourth prime minister. The Canadian Criminal Code is established.
1893	William's family moves to Toronto. William begins his diary on September 6.	An international tribunal decides that Canadians have the right to hunt seals in the Bering Sea.
1894		Sir Mackenzie Bowell becomes the fifth prime minister.
1895	William graduates from the University of Toronto with a BA. He works as a journalist and studies for his law exams.	
1896	William receives his law degree from the University of Toronto. He studies political economy at the University of Chicago.	Sir Charles Tupper becomes the sixth prime minister of Canada. Sir Wilfrid Laurier becomes the seventh prime minister of Canada.
1897	William receives his MA from the University of Toronto. He writes newspaper articles on social problems in Toronto. He starts at Harvard University.	The Klondike gold rush occurs. Clara Brett Martin becomes the first woman admitted to the bar of Ontario. Queen Victoria celebrates her diamond jubilee.
1898	William gets an MA at Harvard. He publishes an investigative report on the working conditions in Boston for the Consumers' League.	The Yukon Territory is formed. The Spanish-American War takes place: Spain loses control of Cuba, Puerto Rico, the Philippines, Guam, and other islands.

48

More on the life and times of William Lyon Mackenzie King

YEAR	WILLIAM'S LIFE	EVENTS IN CANADA AND THE WORLD
1899	William sails for England and begins his studies at the London School of Economics.	The South African War (Boer War) begins (1899–1902): the British win control of what is now the Republic of South Africa. The first Canadian troops are sent to the South African War.
1900	William travels across Europe. He's appointed the deputy minister of the new Department of Labour. He also edits the *Labour Gazette*. He visits Kingsmere, Quebec, for the first time.	The head tax on Chinese immigrants is raised to $100. The Commonwealth of Australia is formed.
1901	William's best friend, Henry Albert Harper, drowns.	The Chinese head tax is raised to $500—the equivalent of two years of labour.
1905		Alberta and Saskatchewan become provinces. The Russian Revolution occurs: Russians protest against the government of Tsar Nicholas II.
1906	William publishes his first book, *The Secret of Heroism*.	
1907		The Industrial Disputes Investigation Act is passed.
1908	William resigns as deputy minister of labour to run for Parliament. He wins a seat in the federal election.	
1909	William becomes the first full-time minister of labour. He receives his Ph.D. from Harvard University.	
1910	William represents Canada at meetings held across Europe.	The Royal Canadian Navy is established.
1911	He loses his seat in the election. He becomes editor of the *Canadian Liberal Monthly*. The Rockefeller Foundation hires him as a consultant.	Sir Robert Laird Borden becomes the eighth prime minister.
1914	William becomes an adviser on industrial relations for the Rockefeller Foundation.	World War I begins in August. The War Measures Act is passed. Canada declares war on Germany in September.
1915	William's sister, Isabel Christina Grace King, dies on April 4.	Canadians fight their first major battle of the war. Known as the Battle of Ypres, in Belgium, it lasts from April 22 to May 25.
1916	William's father, John, dies.	Manitoba amends its Election Act to allow women to vote.
1917	William runs in, and is defeated in, the federal election. The next day his mother, Isabel Grace Mackenzie King, dies.	Canadians fight the Battle of Vimy Ridge in France. A "temporary" income tax is introduced. The National Hockey League (NHL) is formed. The Russian Revolution ends with the Bolsheviks seizing power.
1918	William finishes his work for the Rockefeller Foundation. He publishes his next book, *Industry and Humanity*.	White women are allowed to vote and are eligible to be candidates in all provinces except Prince Edward Island and Quebec. World War I ends on Armistice Day, November 11. A worldwide influenza epidemic kills close to 25 million people.

YEAR	WILLIAM'S LIFE	EVENTS IN CANADA AND THE WORLD
1919	William becomes Liberal leader.	The Winnipeg General Strike occurs from May 15 to June 26. The Treaty of Versailles officially ends World War I.
1920		The League of Nations is established and Canada joins. Arthur Meighen becomes the ninth prime minister. Women become eligible to sit in the House of Commons. The Progressive party forms. The RCMP takes over federal law enforcement.
1921	William becomes the 10th prime minister of Canada and secretary of state for external affairs.	Agnes Macphail is the first woman elected to Parliament.
1922	William's younger brother, Dougall Macdougall, dies.	The Chanak Affair takes place: William delays sending support for British troops in Turkey, insisting it be Parliament's decision. White women are allowed to vote in Prince Edward Island. The Union of Soviet Socialist Republics (USSR) is created.
1923	William moves into Laurier House.	
1924	William receives an Irish terrier named "Pat" as a gift.	The first national postal strike in Canada takes place.
1925	William and the Liberals are defeated in the election but he forms a coalition government with the Progressive party and remains prime minister.	
1926	William wins a by-election, but resigns in June. The Liberals force an election and win. William begins his second term.	Arthur Meighen begins his second term. Old-age pension is introduced.
1929		The Privy Council declares women to be legally "persons." The New York stock market crash triggers the Great Depression.
1930	The Liberals are defeated in the election; William keeps his seat and becomes Opposition leader.	Richard Bedford Bennett becomes the 11th prime minister. Cairine Wilson is the first appointed female senator. Pluto, the ninth planet in the solar system, is discovered.
1932		Co-operative Commonwealth Federation (CCF) party is founded.
1933		Adolf Hitler is appointed chancellor of Germany.
1935	William begins his third term as prime minister. He visits US president Franklin D. Roosevelt.	The Bank of Canada is formed. The RCMP stops the On-to-Ottawa Trek in Regina. Tommy Douglas wins a seat in the CCF party's first election.
1936		The Canadian Broadcasting Corporation (CBC) is created. The Spanish Civil War begins.
1937	William attends the coronation of King George VI in Britain. He travels to Germany and has discussions with Adolf Hitler.	

Even more on the life and times of William Lyon Mackenzie King

YEAR	WILLIAM'S LIFE	EVENTS IN CANADA AND THE WORLD
1939	William signs the British Commonwealth Air Training Plan.	World War II begins when Britain declares war on Germany. Canada declares war on Germany on September 10.
1940	William is declared Canada's wartime leader when he wins the election.	The National Resources Mobilization Act is introduced. White women are given the right to vote in Quebec. Canada declares war on Italy on June 10. Germany invades Holland, Belgium, Luxembourg, and France. Winston Churchill becomes prime minister of Great Britain.
1941	William flies to Great Britain; it's his first flight. William's dog, Pat, dies. He receives a second Irish terrier, whom he names Pat II.	The unemployment insurance program begins. Canadian troops are sent to Hong Kong, which is later captured by Japan; many Canadians perish in battle. British prime minister Winston Churchill visits Ottawa. Japan attacks Pearl Harbor on December 7. Canada, Great Britain, and the United States declare war on Japan.
1942		A national plebiscite on conscription is held. The Progressive and Conservative parties unite to become the Progressive-Conservative (PC) party. Canada and the United States force citizens of Japanese descent to move inland, away from the west coast.
1943	William attends the first Quebec Conference.	Canadian troops invade Sicily, Italy.
1944	William attends the second Quebec Conference.	Ottawa imposes limited conscription for overseas service. The Allies land in Normandy, France, on D-Day, June 6.
1945	William attends the United Nations (UN) conference held in San Francisco. He signs the UN charter as the representative of Canada. William loses his seat but the Liberal party wins the election. He is elected in a by-election.	The Liberal party wins the post-war election. The family-allowance program (baby bonus) begins. The United Nations (UN) is formed and Canada joins. Germany surrenders on May 8. The United States drops two atomic bombs on Japan. Japan surrenders on September 2. The Cold War begins.
1947	William becomes the first official Canadian citizen. His dog, Pat II, dies.	The Canadian Citizenship Act comes into effect.
1948	William resigns as leader of the Liberal party and then as prime minister. He receives his third dog, whom he names Pat III.	Louis St. Laurent becomes the 12th prime minister. South Africa introduces apartheid. A war between Israel and Arab forces from Egypt, Syria, Transjordan (later Jordan), Lebanon, and Iraq begins.
1949	William does not run in the election.	Newfoundland becomes a province. The North Atlantic Treaty Organization (NATO) is created. The Supreme Court becomes the final court of appeal. Canada joins NATO.
1950	William dies on July 22 in Kingsmere, Quebec. He is buried in Mount Pleasant Cemetery, Toronto.	The Korean War begins: North Korea invades South Korea. When the fighting ends, the two countries remain divided and officially still at war. No peace agreement has been reached.

51

Glossary: words and facts you might want to know

Allies: term used to describe the countries that fought against the Axis countries during World War II. The Allied countries were Great Britain, France, the United States, the USSR, Canada, and Australia. The Axis was an alliance between Germany, Italy, and, later, Japan.

anti-Semitism: literally means "opposition to Semites." Semites are Middle Eastern peoples who trace their origin from the Biblical figure Noah and his son Shem; these include Jews and Arabs. However, the term is almost always applied specifically to the hatred, prejudice, oppression, or discrimination against Jews or Judaism.

Bennett, Richard Bedford (1870–1947): Canada's 11th prime minister (1930–1935). Born in New Brunswick and trained as a lawyer. He became involved in politics first as a member of the assembly of the Northwest Territories. He became prime minister during the very difficult Great Depression.

Borden, Sir Robert Laird (1854–1937): defeated Sir Wilfrid Laurier and the Liberals to become Canada's eighth prime minister (1911–1920). He was born in Nova Scotia and worked as a teacher before becoming a lawyer.

by-election: an election that takes place in a single riding when the person who has represented that riding has resigned or died. It can happen at federal, provincial, and municipal levels of government.

Byng of Vimy, Julian Hedworth George, Viscount (1862–1935): British governor general of Canada (1921–1926). He was a British aristocrat and cavalry offi-

cer. In 1926, he refused to dissolve King's government after it had been defeated in a confidence vote. As a result, King resigned and Arthur Meighen was asked to form a new government.

Cold War (1945–1990): the struggle that developed between the USSR and the other Allies after World War II. It was called the "Cold War" because it didn't lead to widespread fighting (or a "hot war"). Each side accused the other of wanting to rule the world.

concentration camps: a place where political prisoners and members of national or minority groups are confined for reasons of state security, exploitation, or punishment. During World War II, the first German concentration camps were set up in 1933 to confine opponents of the Nazi party: communists and social democrats. This group soon grew to include Jews, gypsies, homosexuals, and anti-Nazi civilians from the occupied territories.

confidence vote: a special vote in the House of Commons that a minority government must win to stay in power. If the government does not win the vote, it has lost the confidence of the House. This is called a vote of non-confidence and the government usually resigns or asks the governor general to dissolve Parliament and call an election. Votes on the Speech from the Throne, and tax and spending bills, are automatically considered to be confidence votes. Voting on any major bill that reflects the government's program can be, too. The Opposition can also introduce a minor motion or an amendment to a motion that explicitly says the

government does not have the confidence of the House. The House then votes on it.

Conservative Party of Canada: the first party to govern the Dominion of Canada. It began in 1854 when politicians from Upper and Lower Canada joined to form a coalition government of the Province of Canada. Sir John A. Macdonald was its first leader.

constitution: the highest set of laws in a country. Just like you have rules in your home to help take care of your property, relationships, and personal well-being, a constitution is a set of laws or rules that lays out how a government must take care of its people, and the rights these people can expect their government to protect. Most countries have written constitutions that set out the basic laws of their state.

D-Day: the first day of the Allied landing in Normandy, France, during World War II. It took place on June 6, 1944. The landing was the starting point of the massive push eastward through France to Nazi Germany.

Fascism: a political system led by a single dictator who allows no opposition. The nation is the highest priority, instead of individual freedoms. It is used to describe the nationalistic and totalitarian regimes of Benito Mussolini (Italy, 1922–1945), Adolf Hitler (Germany, 1933–1945), and Francisco Franco (Spain, 1939–1975).

family allowance: also known as the "baby bonus," these were monthly payments to help sup-

More words and facts you might want to know

port all dependent children up to the age of 18 years. It began in Canada in 1945.

governor general: the representative of the King or Queen in Canada who provides the royal assent necessary for all laws passed by Parliament. The governor general is a figurehead who performs only symbolic, formal, ceremonial, and cultural duties, and whose job is to encourage Canadian excellence, identity, unity, and leadership.

Great Depression (1929–1939): also known as "The Dirty Thirties," this was a worldwide economic slump. The cause is still being debated by experts. Two catastrophes happened right before the Depression: an enormous loss of the wheat crop in 1928 and the stock market crash in October 1929. Many people were out of work and money and food supplies began to run low. This Depression affected everyone in some way and there was no way to escape it.

Harper, Henry Albert (Bert) (1875–1901): William's closest friend. They met while studying at the University of Toronto. Bert died tragically during a skating party on the Ottawa River. He jumped into the river to save someone who fell through thin ice. Unfortunately, the current was too strong for Bert and both of them drowned.

Hitler, Adolf (1889–1945): ruled Germany as dictator from 1933 to 1945. Although born in Austria, he served in World War I as a messenger in the German army. He joined a group that became the National Socialist German Workers' party,

also known as the Nazi party. After he led the Nazi party to power in 1933, he prepared the country for war. World War II began in 1939 and ended a week after he killed himself, in 1945. He was responsible for the deaths of millions of people in the concentration camps that he set up.

House of Commons: the lower house of Parliament. It consists of a speaker, the prime minister and his cabinet, members of the governing party, members of the opposition parties, and sometimes a few independent members (elected members who do not belong to an official party). The members of the House (called members of Parliament or MPs) are elected in constituency elections or by-elections by the Canadian people. The House (often incorrectly referred to as Parliament) is important because it is where all new laws start.

industrialization: the gradual change of a society's economy and culture when its population moves from farming to factory work. Large numbers of workers (and often their families) leave rural farming areas for industrial towns and cities. Inventions such as the steam engine, the weaving machine, and steel making are credited with starting the process in 16th-century England.

internment camps: detention or confinement centres for civilians during wars. Detainees are denied certain legal rights, like the ability to question the legality of their arrest. During the two world wars, Canada interned enemy aliens and Canadian citizens. There were various types of these camps. Some were groups of buildings

surrounded by barbed wire and armed guards. Some were whole towns, complete with schools for interned children. And some were just shelters or tents to house people who'd been forced to work on roads or farms.

King, Dougall Macdougall (1878–1922): William's younger brother. He was known as "Max" or "Mac" to family and friends. He became a doctor and served in the medical corps of the Canadian forces fighting in the Boer War. He developed tuberculosis and had little hope of recovering. Max did recover but fell ill two years later with a muscle disease. He eventually became paralyzed and died at the age of 44.

King, Isabel Christina Grace (1873–1915): William's older sister. Bella, as she was called, started training as a nurse but William (and their father) didn't approve and convinced her to stop. She started to study home economics but had to quit to care for her mother who was suffering from the flu. Bella never married and spent much of her time caring for her aging parents.

King, Isabel Grace Mackenzie (1843–1917): daughter of the leader of the Rebellion of 1837, William Lyon Mackenzie, and the mother of William Lyon Mackenzie King. She and her husband, John King, had four children: Bella, William, Janet, and Macdougall. William and his mother were very close. After he became established in Ottawa, she visited him often. William idolized her, even after her death.

More words and facts you might want to know

King, Janet Lindsey (1876–1962): known as "Jennie," she was William's younger sister. In the late 1940s, Jennie helped to restore Woodside, one of her childhood homes, made famous because William was prime minister.

King, John (1843–1916): William's father. He was a lawyer in Berlin (now Kitchener), Ontario. In 1872, he married Isabel Grace Mackenzie. In 1893, the family moved to Toronto, where John worked as a lawyer, lecturer, and writer. In his later years, his eyesight began to fail, and he became nearly blind.

Laurier, Sir Wilfrid (1841–1911): Canada's seventh prime minister and the first one who was a French Canadian.

Liberal Party of Canada: the second party to govern the Dominion of Canada. The party was formed in 1867, after Confederation. Canada's second prime minister was a Liberal, Sir Alexander Mackenzie.

Macdonald, Sir John A. (1815–1891): Canada's first prime minister (1867–1873, 1878–1891). Born in Scotland, he moved to Upper Canada with his family in 1820. He trained and worked as a lawyer before becoming involved in politics. He spent many years working on bringing the Province of Canada and the Maritime provinces together. On July 1, 1867, his dream came true with the creation of the Dominion of Canada. He died while in office in Ottawa.

Mackenzie, William Lyon (1795–1861): leader of the Upper Canada Rebellion in 1837. First elected to the Legislative Assembly of Upper Canada, he later became the first mayor of Toronto. After an unsuccessful attempt to overthrow the government of Upper Canada, Mackenzie escaped to the United States, where he set up a provisional government.

Meighen, Arthur (1874–1960): Canada's ninth prime minister (1920–1921, June–September 1926). Born in Ontario, he worked as a teacher and a salesman before moving to Manitoba and training as a lawyer. In 1908, he was elected to the House of Commons and, in 1920, he succeeded Sir Robert Borden as prime minister. After the King-Byng affair, he retired from politics, only to return in 1932 when he was appointed to the Senate.

Mulroney, Brian (1939–): Canada's 18th prime minister (1984–1993). Mulroney was born in Quebec to Irish immigrants, and trained as a lawyer. He specialized in labour negotiations and eventually became president of a mining company. Without ever having run for office, Mulroney became leader of the Progressive Conservative (PC) party in 1983. In 1984, he led the PCs to win the most seats (211) in Canadian history.

New World: the continents of North and South America. This term has been used since the 1500s, when the Americas were first explored and colonized by Europeans. Before their discovery of the New World, Europeans used to think the earth consisted only of Europe, Asia, and Africa (the Old World).

old-age pension: payments made to older citizens to make sure that they have some income in order to live. The first old-age pension act was passed into law in 1927.

Pasteur, Louis (1822–1895): from France, he developed a way to keep milk, wine, beer, and food from spoiling. First he noticed that germs caused food and drink to spoil. Then he figured out that heating them up just enough would kill the germs. This process became known as pasteurization. He also invented vaccines to prevent diseases.

propaganda: speaking or writing that tries to convince people to accept a certain point of view by using one-sided rather than objective arguments. It is sometimes used as a form of political or religious advertisement. It can also be used by companies to convince people to buy their products, such as toys or candy, on television, billboards, and the like.

racism: a form of discrimination based on race, especially the belief that one race is superior to another. It happens when people mistreat, discriminate against, dislike, hate, or judge other people based on their race.

Rebellion of 1837: uprising against the government of Upper Canada led by William Lyon Mackenzie. Some people were fed up with the government and wanted to make it more democratic for all people. On December 5, 1837, about 800 angry men marched down Yonge Street in Toronto to try to take over the legislature and set up their own government. They were fired on by a small group of defenders and fled

Still more words and facts you might want to know

back the way they had come. This rebellion immediately followed the more violent rebellion that took place in Lower Canada. Mackenzie was trying to take advantage of the fact that British troops had left Toronto to defend the government of Lower Canada.

Rockefeller Foundation: a global non-profit organization that began in 1913 to make lasting improvements in the lives of poor people throughout the world. It was started by John D. Rockefeller, who was, at one time, the world's richest person.

seat in Parliament: place where an elected member of Parliament sits in the House of Commons, part of Canada's Parliament. Parliament is the national legislature of Canada. It has two houses, an upper house called the Senate and a lower house called the House of Commons. Senators are appointed by the governor general but the Canadian people elect their representatives in the House of Commons.

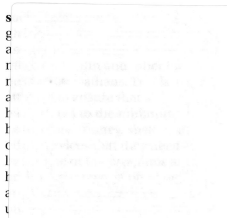

s
g
a
n
n
a
h
h
c
l
h
a
u
pension, and family allowance.

stock market crash: on Black Tuesday, October 29, 1929, in New York, Toronto, Montreal, and other financial centres in the world, as

prices began to drop, shareholders panicked and sold their stocks for whatever they could get before they became worthless. Prices on the stock market collapsed completely. Most of the people and businesses that had borrowed money to buy the stocks couldn't pay back their loans to the banks. Millions of people lost every cent they had. Most banks failed, factories shut down, stores closed, and governments couldn't collect their tax money to pay for services. Massive unemployment followed. It was an economic disaster that caused (or was a major contributing factor of) the Great Depression, a 10-year economic slump affecting all Western industrialized countries.

Third Reich: the official Nazi term for the government of Germany from January 1933 to May 1945. The First Reich lasted from 800 to 1806 during the medieval and early modern Holy Roman Empire eras. The Second Reich was the name given to the German Empire from 1871 to 1918.

unemployment insurance (UI): government benefits paid when people are unemployed. The program began to operate in 1941 in Canada. To qualify for benefits, applicants must prove that they were previously employed for a certain amount of time. The program's name has been changed to "employment insurance" (EI).

United Nations (UN): an organization that works for international peace and security. The UN provides a place for countries to meet and settle their problems peacefully. It was established in 1945 at the end of World War II. Its headquarters is in New York City, with

an office in Geneva, Switzerland, and agencies throughout the world. Fifty-one countries joined the UN when it started (including Canada and the United States) and over 70 more have signed on since.

Upper Canada (1791–1841): province created by the Constitutional Act of 1791, which divided the former Province of Quebec into two parts: Upper Canada and Lower Canada. These two provinces were joined once again to form the Province of Canada in 1841 and were also known as Canada West (Upper Canada, or Ontario) and Canada East (Lower Canada, or Quebec).

World War I (1914–1918): also known as the First World War, or the Great War. It was an international conflict that involved most of the countries of Europe as well as Russia, the United States, the Middle East, and other regions. The war pitted the Central Powers—mainly Germany, Austria-Hungary, and Turkey—against the Allies—mainly France, Great Britain (including Canada), Russia, Italy, Japan, and, from 1917, the United States. It ended with the defeat of the Central Powers.

World War II (1939–1945): a conflict that involved almost every part of the world. The main participants were the Axis powers—Germany, Italy, and Japan—and the Allies—France, Great Britain (including Canada and Australia), the United States, and the USSR. The war was a continuation of problems that were left unresolved by World War I. It was the largest war in history and ended with the defeat of the Axis countries.

For more information on the terms listed in this glossary, visit www.jackfruitpress.com

Index